KITTY CAPERS

CARTOONS & JOKES
FOR CAT LOVERS EVERYWHERE

By Joel Rothman

Published in the UK by
POWERFRESH Limited
Unit 3 Everdon Park
Heartlands Business Park
Daventry
NN11 8YJ

Telephone 01327 871 777
Facsimile   01327 879 222
E Mail   info@powerfresh.co.uk

Copyright © 2005 Joel Rothman
Cover and interior layout by Powerfresh

ISBN   1904967299

All rights reserved. No part of this publication may be reproduced or transmitted in any form or by any means, electronic or mechanical, including photocopying, recording or any information storage and retrieval system, or for the source of ideas without the written permission of the publisher.

Printed in The UK by Belmont Press
Powerfresh   October 2005

For Melissa
and her cat,
Treacle

Walking by a pet shop can make some people very emotional. You hear the scratching against the window, the meowing, the pleading eyes — and that's just the owner!

The old millionaire didn't want to be too obvious, so in his will he wrote: "To my beloved cat, Matilda, I leave my entire fortune. And to my loyal secretary, Miss Foster, I leave my cat."

I washed my cat the other day and she really enjoyed it —— I did, too, if only her fur didn't stick to the roof of my mouth!

A Dog Thinks: These people I live with feed me, love me, provide me with a warm and dry home, pet me and take good care of me—they must be gods.

A Cat Thinks: These people I live with feed me, love me, provide me with a warm and dry home, pet me and take good care of me — I must be God.

A husband walked in the house and told his wife, "The cat from next door won't dig up the vegetables in our garden anymore — I just cut off its tail."

That's a horrible thing to do!" said the shocked wife. "And besides, how will that stop her from getting into our garden?"

"It will, it will," explained the husband, "you see — I snipped off the tail — at the neck!"

I took my sick cat to a vet. The vet shot him—it was a Vietnam vet.

They were devoted to each other, so I had Marion put down when Fluffy died.

Ivan's teacher asked, "How was your weekend?"

"Horrible—a car hit my cat in the ass."

"Rectum," said the teacher. "You should say rectum."

"Rectum?" replied Ivan. "Why it damn near killed him!"

Before a cat will condescend to treat you as a trusted friend, some little token of esteem is needed, like a dish of cream.

T.S. Eliot

How did you get on in the milk-drinking competition?
It was a cinch — I won by six laps!

IF A CAT'S PRAYERS WERE ANSWERED IT WOULD RAIN MICE.

When you sold me this cat you said it would be good for mice — but she won't go near them!
FRANK'S PETS
Well, isn't that good for mice?

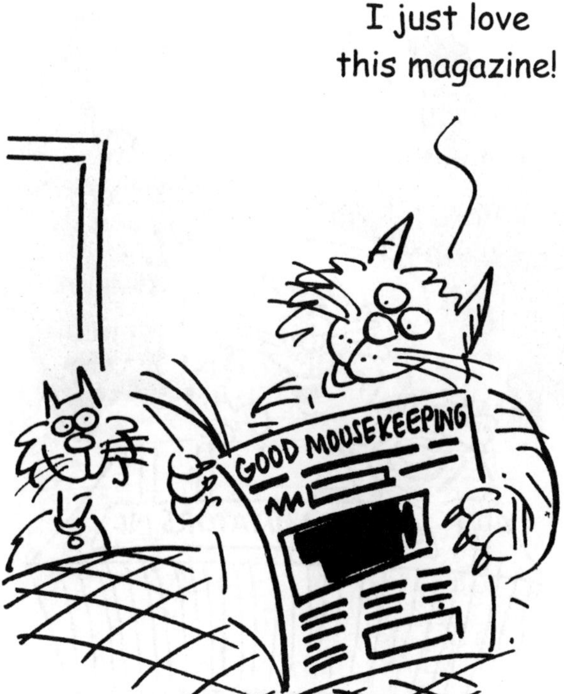
I just love this magazine!
GOOD MOUSEKEEPING

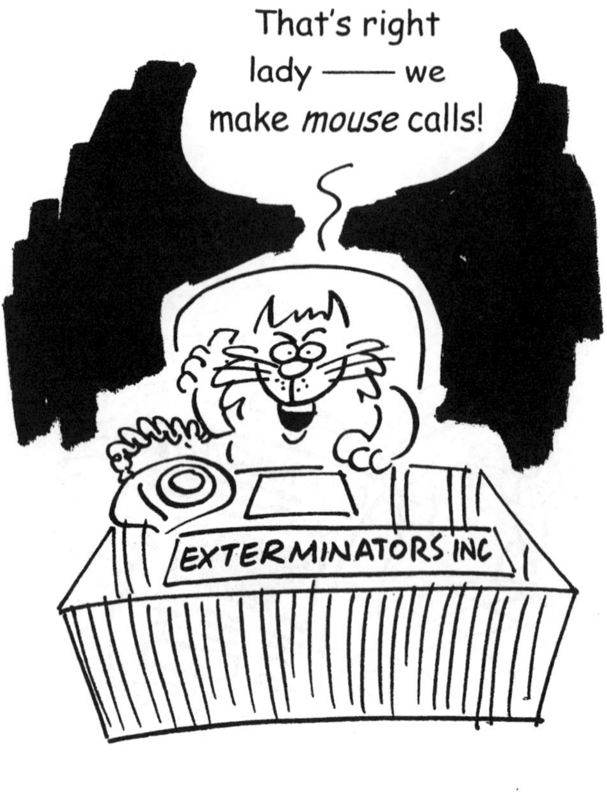
That's right lady —— we make *mouse* calls!
EXTERMINATORS INC

Have you been eating cheese?
Yeah, now I'm waiting for a mouse with baited breath!

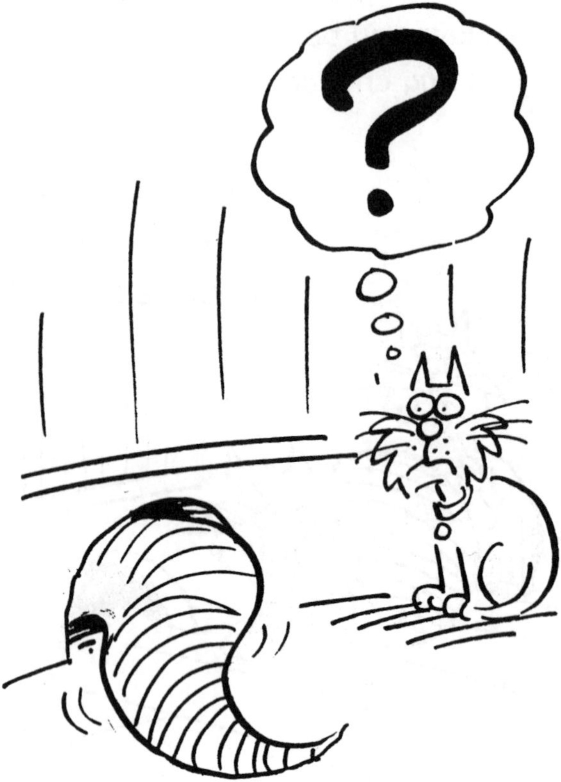

I haven't eaten a juicy, fat mouse in ages!

Here kitty, kitty!

It's for you!

AN ALLEY CAT ALSO HAS
NINE WIVES

Come on —— don't be afraid —— after all we only have nine lives . . .

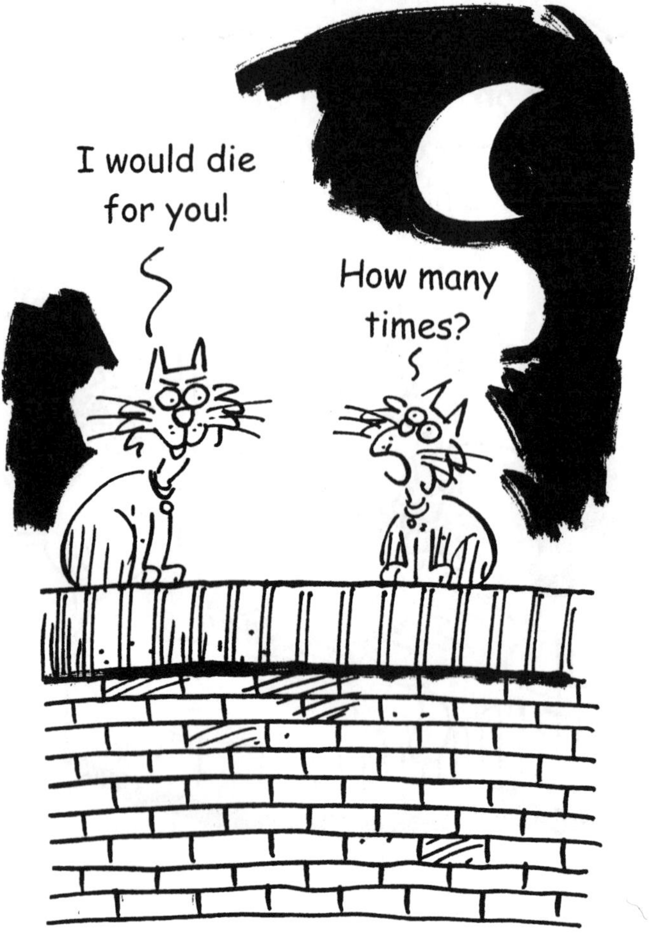
I would die for you!
How many times?

As the castrated alley cat said, "Me-how?"

I saw your cat running around the street like mad!
I know —— he's just been neutered and he's rushing around cancelling engagements!

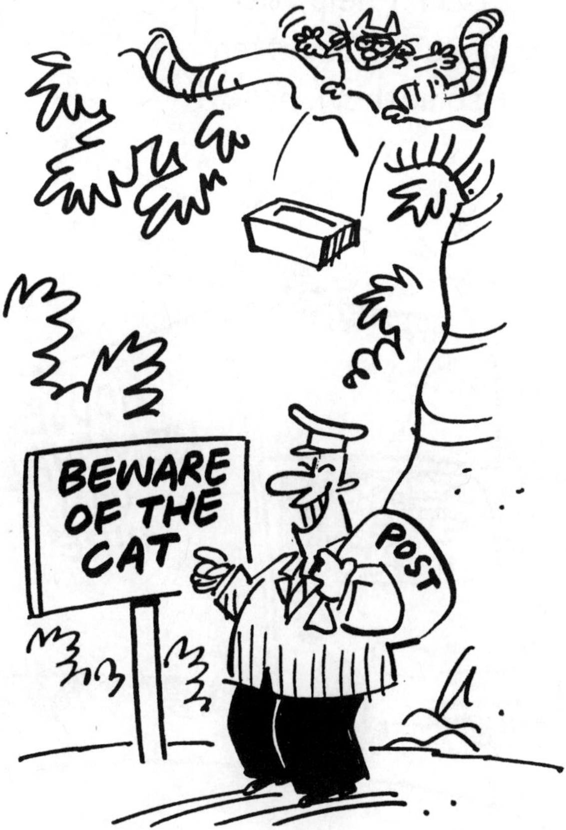
BEWARE OF THE CAT
POST

I can't help feeling
we've forgotten
something, honey!

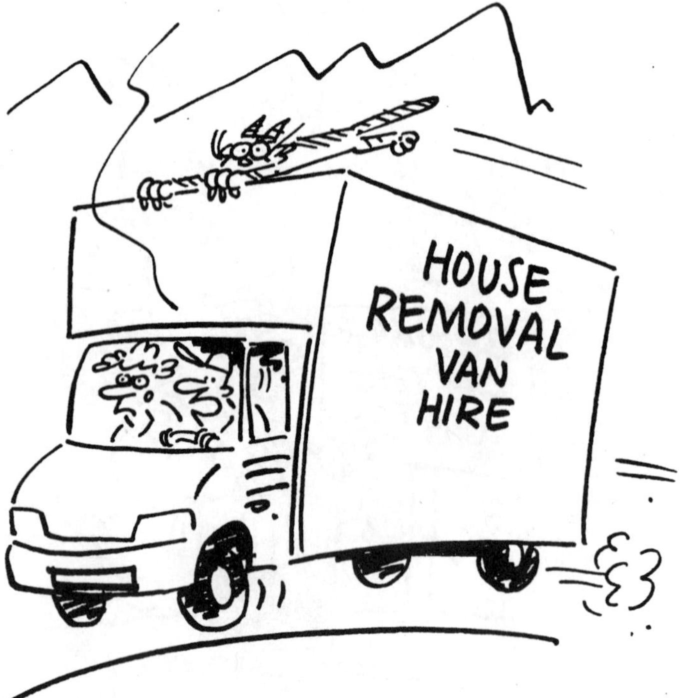

This is a large impersonal city —— Joel and I have been living here for over a year and we still don't know our neighbors. But our cat is OK —— already she's had two litters!

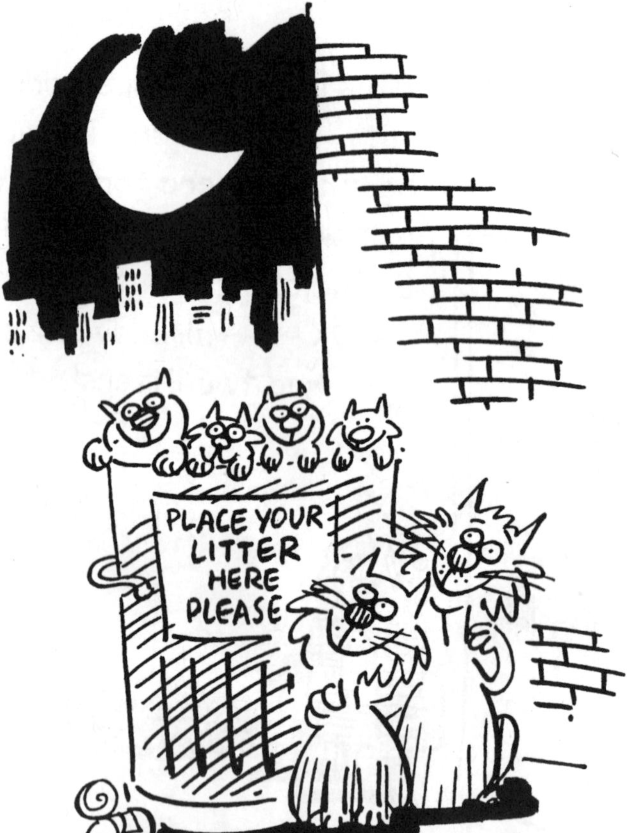
PLACE YOUR
LITTER
HERE
PLEASE

Jeeves —— I saw a mouse in the kitchen!
Very good, Madam —— I'll see if the cat is available to dine.

Pussycat, Pussycat where have you been?
I've been to London to see the Queen!
Name — dropper!

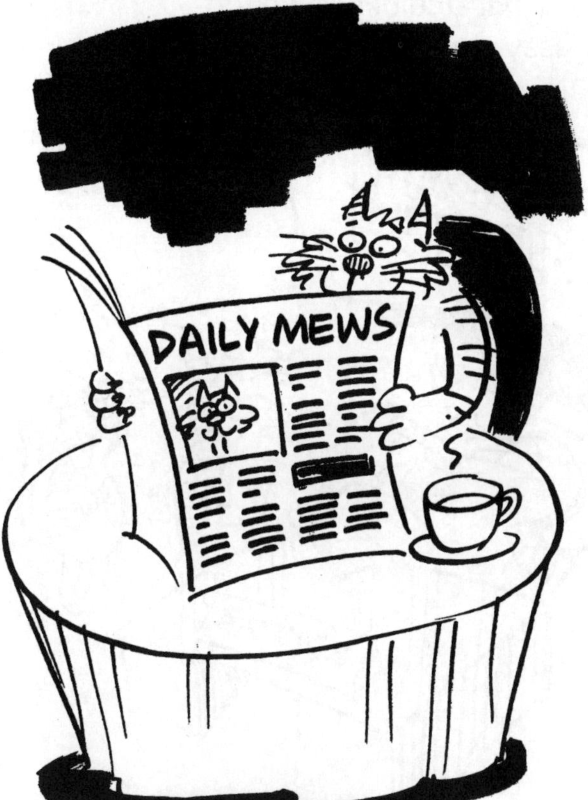
DAILY MEWS

Say —— he's looking particularly pleased with himself!
He should —— he's just won the *purr*litzer prize!
SUNDAY MEWS
EDITOR

She can't look at my cat —— I think she's got *purr*anoia.

THE FELINE PSYCHIATRIST WAS KNOWN AS A FREUDY CAT . . .

"I washed my cat last night and it died."
"But washing a cat can't kill it."
"Well, it was either the washing or the spin dryer that did it!"

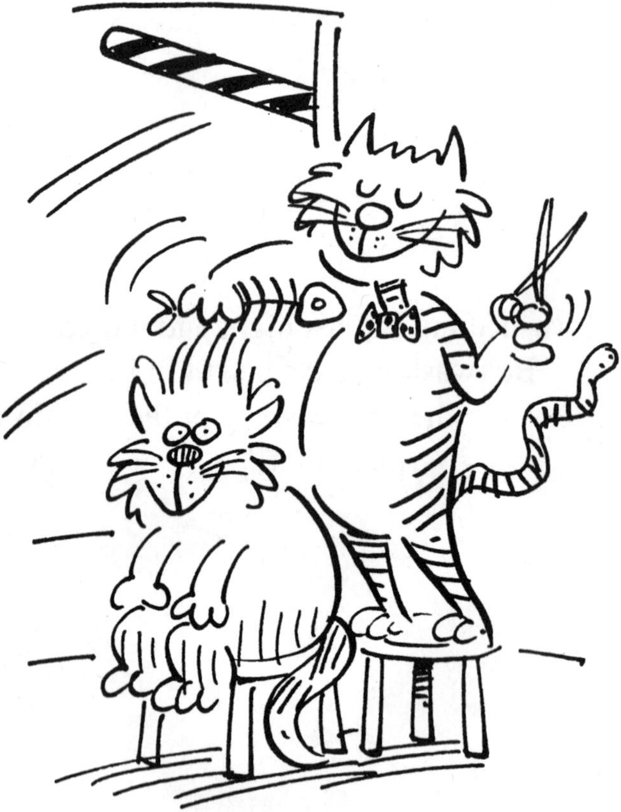

You've been away for over a month — naturally she's upset!

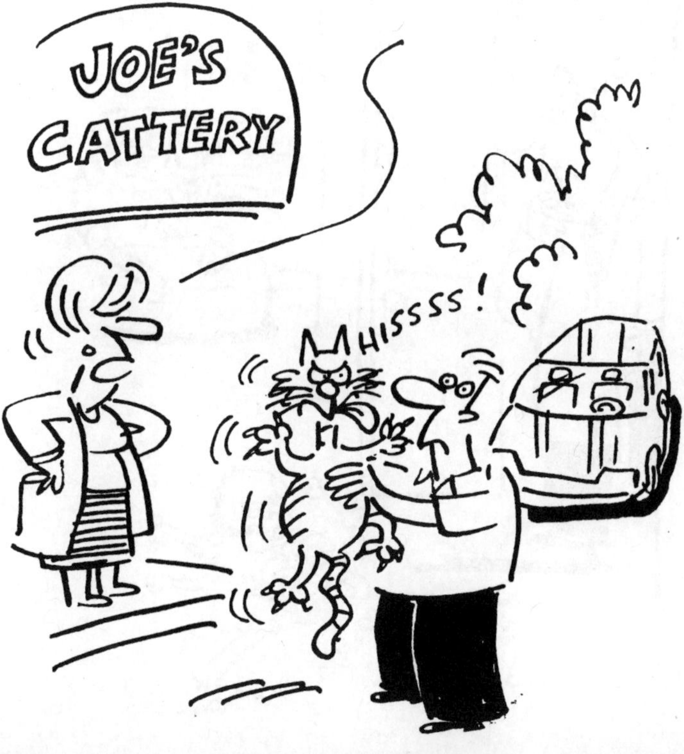

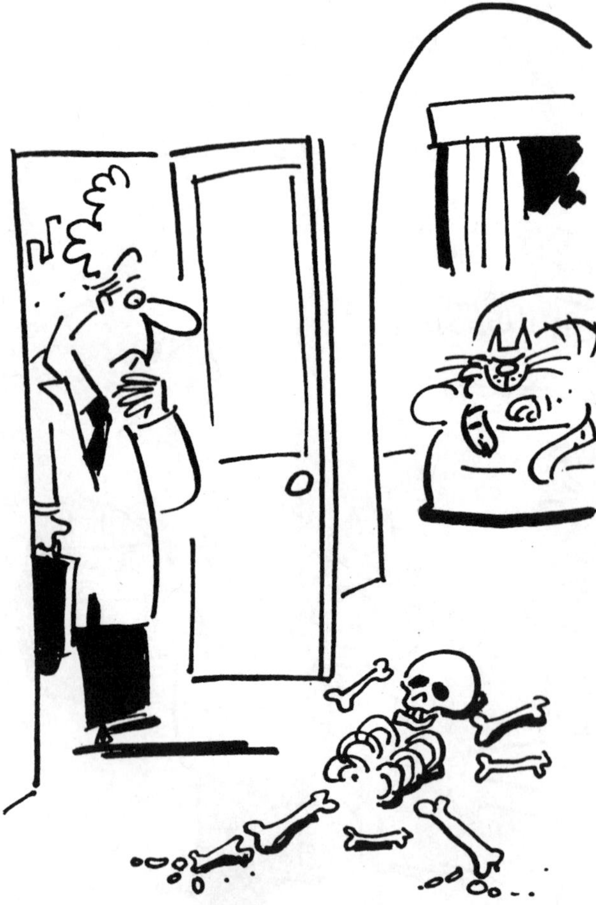

My wife has always wanted a jaguar, so I finally bought her one —— that same night it ate her up!

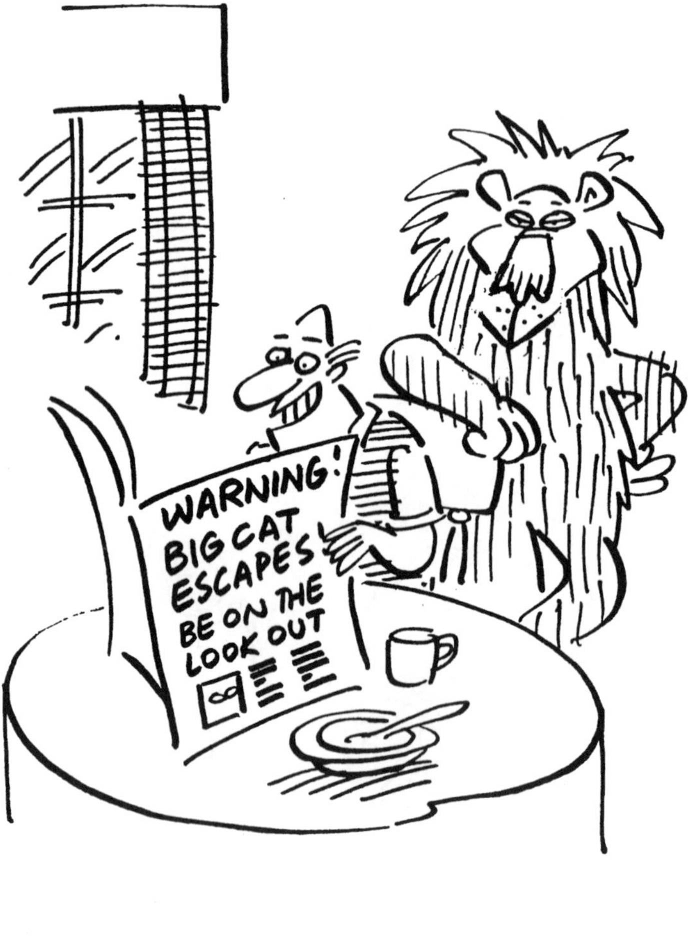
WARNING!
BIG CAT
ESCAPES!
BE ON THE
LOOK OUT

In a schoolroom in Cuba, young Carmen was asked to say a sentence containing a dependent clause.

"The cat had a litter of four kittens," she answered, "all of which are good communists."

"Wonderful," praised the teacher.

Two weeks later Fidel Castro came to visit the class, and the teacher called on Carmen. When asked to give a sentence with a dependent clause, the young student said, "The cat had a litter of four kittens, all of which are good democratic capitalists."

"How could you say a thing like that?" demanded the embarrassed teacher. "Two weeks ago you didn't give me that answer."

"That's true," replied Carmen, "but my kitten's eyes are now wide open."

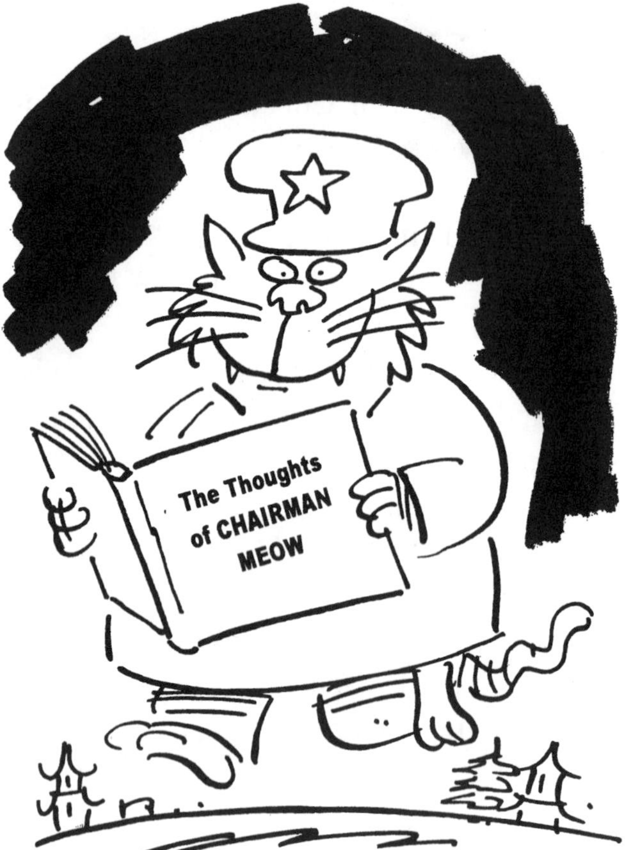
The Thoughts of CHAIRMAN MEOW

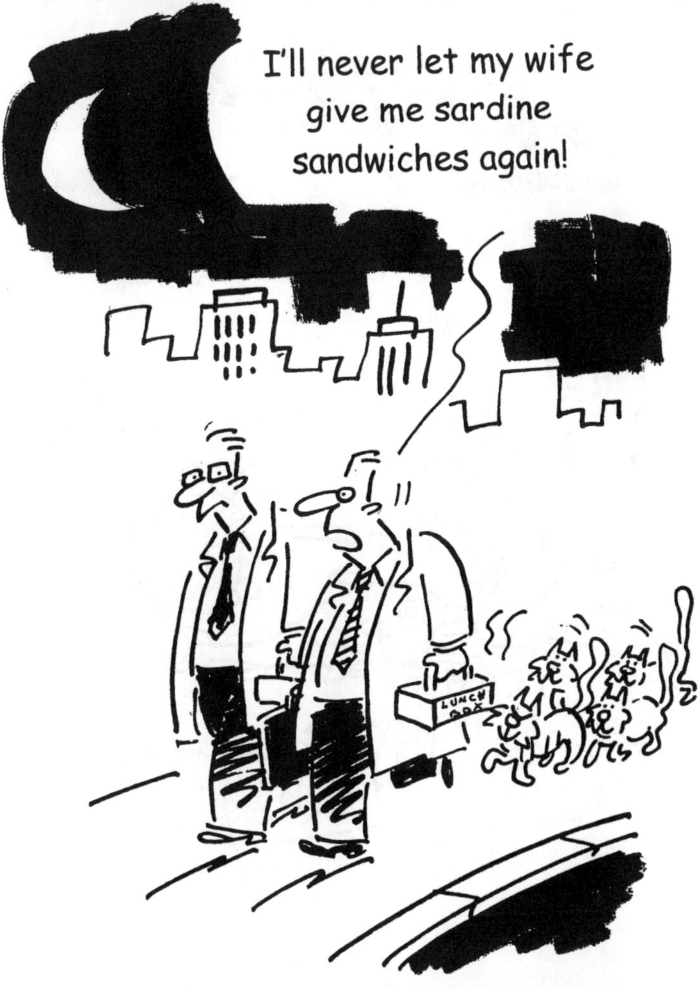
I'll never let my wife give me sardine sandwiches again!

Heads or tails?

Cats have nine lives—which makes them ideal for experimental research.

This is no exaggeration —— my wife is such a bad cook that the cat only has three lives left.

A young women was terribly fond of her pet cat, but it darted into the street one day and was killed by a passing motorist. Her husband came home from work and found her crying hysterically.
"Tell me what happened?"
"Our Ruby was run over and now she's dead," sobbed the wife.
The husband tried to comfort her.
"Now, now," he said, "calm down and I'll buy you another cat."
"Another cat!" screamed the wife. "why, if you realised how much I adored Ruby, you'd buy me a fur coat!"

I'm sorry to hear your two cats have died —— would you like them mounted?
TAXIDERMIST
STAFF ONLY
No —— just holding hands!

Assume your cat owns you if:

1) You keep a picture of the cat in your wallet and you take it out when friends show pictures of their children.
2) You kiss your cat on the lips.
3) Your cat sits at the table when you eat.
4) You feed your cat tidbits from the table.
5) You spend more on a Christmas present for your cat than you do for your partner.
6) You refuse to date anyone who doesn't own a cat.
7) Before considering any relationship you insist both of you bring along their cats to see if they get along.
8) When people phone you insist they say a few words to the cat.

After my Fifi died I
swore I'd never get
another cat!

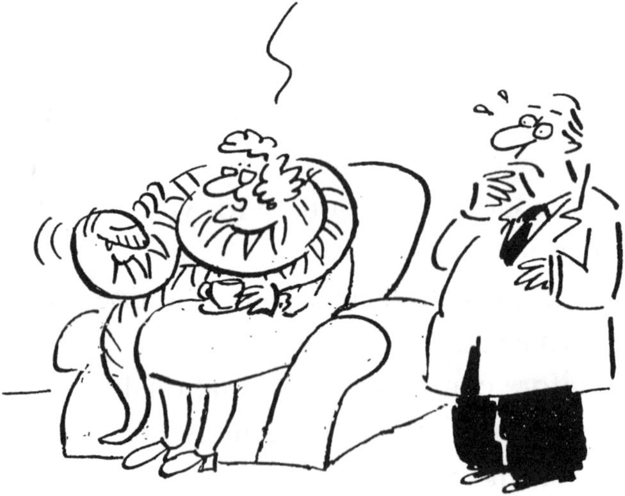

What do you mean
you love me —
you can't even see
what I look like!

I'd hate to think this was just another shipboard romance!
NOAH'S ARK

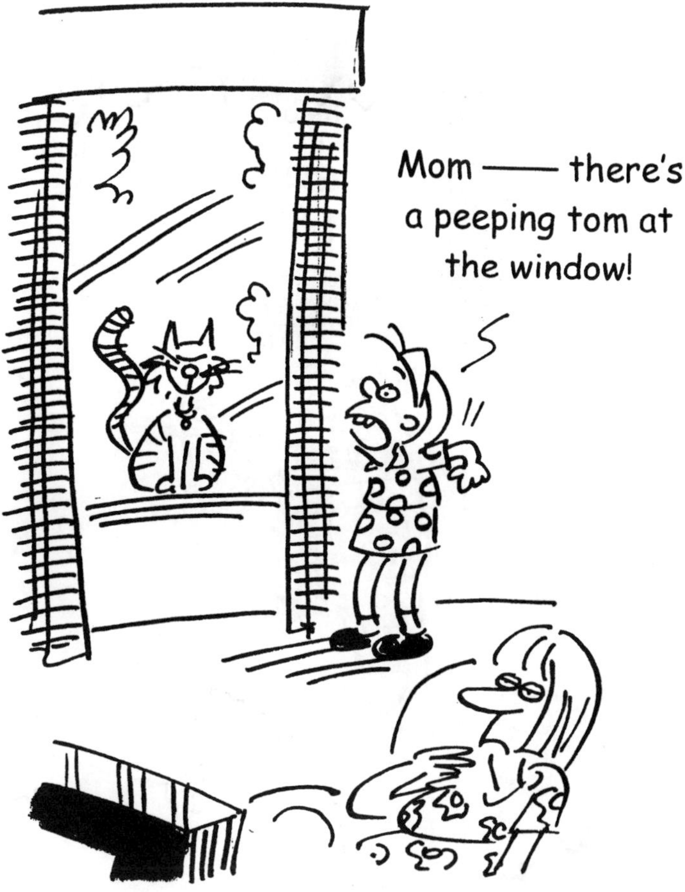
Mom —— there's a peeping tom at the window!

A PURRRFECT MATCH

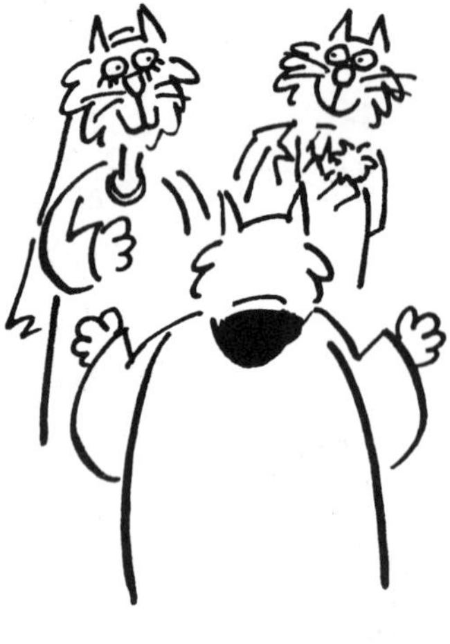

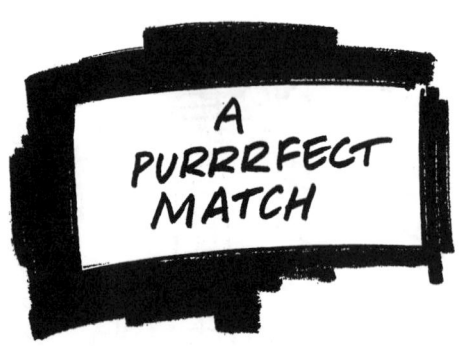